SOMETHING FISH

The Angle from PUNCH

Edited by William Hewison

A PUNCH BOOK

Published in association with

GRAFTON BOOKS

A Division of the Collins Publishing Group

LONDON GLASGOW
TORONTO SYDNEY AUCKLAND

Grafton Books
A Division of the Collins Publishing Group
8 Grafton Street, London W1X 3LA

Published by Grafton Books 1990

British Library Cataloguing in Publication Data

Something fishy: The angle from Punch.
1. English humorous cartoons
I. Hewison, William
741.5942

ISBN 0-246-13647-2

Printed in Great Britain by
William Collins Sons & Co. Ltd, Glasgow

Introduction

I have to confess, as someone who does not spend a lot of time in pursuit of gastronomic delights, that I have never actually seen one of these things *in situ* so to speak. My knowledge of their existence comes partly from occasional glimpses of them in feature films but to a much greater extent from their regular appearance in cartoon drawings. What I'm on about are those tanks of lobsters and other fishy creatures which seem to be a standard fitting in the smarter type of eatery. The diner points to a victim, the waiter plies his scoop, the chef turns up the gas, and a ritual of dubious practicality is completed.

I also have the notion that cartoonists, like me, have latched on to this culinary performance probably at second hand, but because they are experienced professionals they recognise that here they have been presented with a colourful scenario ripe for exploitation, and exploit they certainly do.

On the other hand, the ordinary business of catching fish in the first place – from sea or river – seems not to have gripped their attention much at all, maybe because someone sitting immobile for hours on end with nothing happening is a right turn-off when it comes to comic inspiration. I have the impression that cartoonists on the whole do not go fishing, despite the statistic which informs us that today angling is by far the most popular of sports. When it comes to leisure activity cartoonists tend to be more familiar with the billiard cue than with the fishing rod.

But it was not always so; one hundred years ago the pages of *Punch* were littered with well-off townies casting their lines into Scottish rivers, attended by pawky Scottish gillies at the ready with advice. As one such episode had it:

> English Angler (*on this side of the Tweed*): 'Hi, Donald! Come over and help me land him – a 20-pounder I'll swear –' Highlander (*on the other*): 'It wull tak' ye a lang time to lan' that fush too, sir, whatever! Ye hae hooked the kingdom o' auld Scotland!'

Nowadays, to my knowledge Merrily Harpur and Norman Thelwell are the only *Punch* cartoonists who regularly don the waders and cast the fly, so when they hook a funny idea the drawing stands authentically as a despatch from the sharp end where it is all happening. The cliché of the boasting angler with his arms outstretched is not for them.

Still, there's more to fishing than that, so we mustn't forget the vasty waters of the oceans and the fact that some of these *Punch* cartoonists have ventured thereon, most frequently in the company of Mr Melville and his Great White Whale, where their reports on the latest exploits of Captain Ahab and his crew have got more and more fantastical and zany as the years roll by. As 'Moby Dick' has always sounded like a character from a comic, then that's OK.

Be all that as it may, it must be acknowledged that these workaday humorists are happier and more comfortably lodged in their own homes, where cod comes with chips, where goldfish swim in diddy little bowls, where prowling sharks and lurking octopods are safely corralled behind the TV screen. Fish in themselves, it must be recognised, are hardly bursting with character and personality; even so our comic artists have met the challenge, and in their usual skilful and imaginative way they have netted a weighty catch.

William Hewison

"Where's that waiter with our fish course?"

"I'm fairly philosophical about being boiled. What I object to is being dressed."

"Of course they're chewy – you're supposed to take the peel off."

"It had to happen one day, Jacques – they're getting used to us."

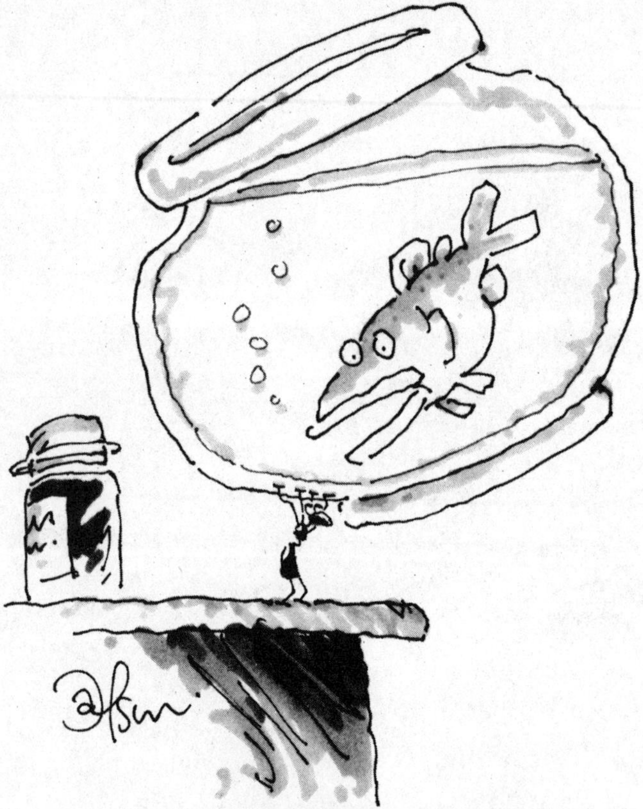

"I swear, I didn't realise – I thought it was caviar."

"Her canapés are not up to the usual standard."

"Did you know that the most popular sport in Britain is buying equipment?"

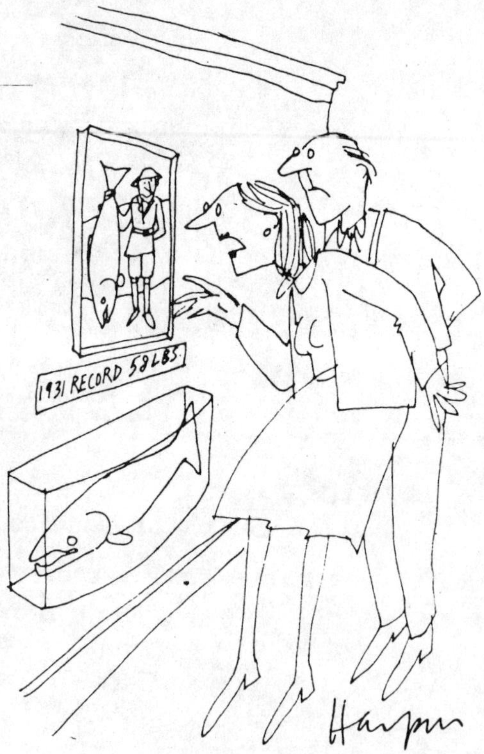

"That must be the smallest man ever to catch a salmon!"

"My God! That joke is 3,000,000 years old and formerly thought to be extinct."

NOT YET
Arnold WILES.

THE
ANGLERS
ARMS
THE
ANGLERS
ARMS
Arnold
Wiles

"Now I see it close up, it's really more of a dirty grey colour!"

"Well, at least we've got more room than the poor sods in the other tank."

"Good luck, men – I hope you have a good catch."

"On the other hand, they may be decoys."

"No, no, lad! Just mark up the new prices on each tank."

"Well, you're not leaving until we get that scallop shell back – they're not ten-a-penny you know!"

"Excuse me, do you happen to have seen a white whale?"

"That's how it is, kids. Birds gotta swim, fish gotta fly."

"Remember, Catto contains every food ingredient that your cat needs!"

"If you think I'm going to knock myself out to have your kids, you're crazy."

"Bloody telly's overheating again, dear."

"Drop it!"

"How vulgar! It's not as if they were fly-fishing."

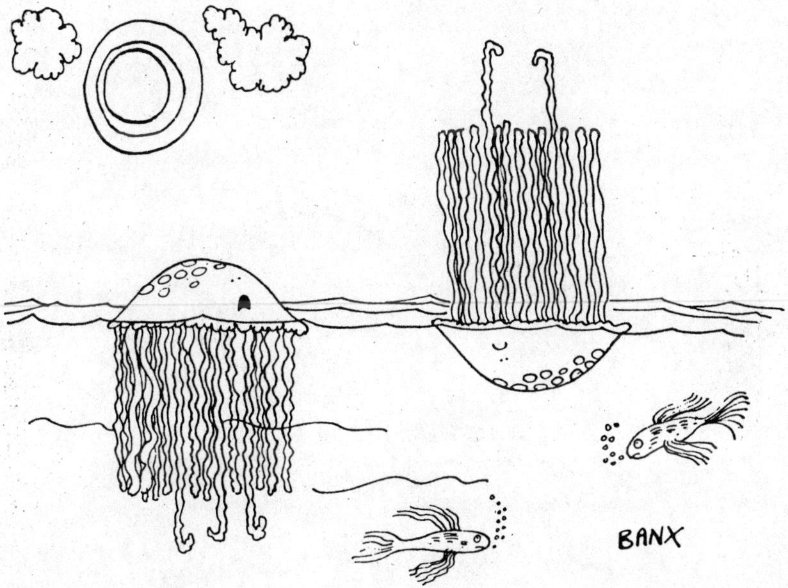

"The first thing you've got to learn is to relax."

HARGREAVES.

ANGLING CLUB
OF
GREAT BRITAIN

THE ANGLER
HADDOCK OF THE MONTH
albert.

NO, NO! NOT ME!
NOT ME!
I'M TOO YOUNG!
NO! NO!
TAKE HIM!
Cotham

JWTAYLOR

"Guess what's behind me in the food chain – bloody pussy cats!"

YOU'VE SEEN
THE FILM!
...NOW TRY
THE SOUP!
SHARK'S FIN
Harper

"He doesn't seem any happier than when he was in his little bowl."

"Ah – here comes your 'Fruits of the Sea' starter."

"But surely there's more to life than playing bridge all day."

"I was quite a normal fish when I was young, then one day an aircraft carrying nuclear bombs crashed into the sea."

"He's a very lucky goldfish."

thelwell

IN CASE OF FIRE BREAK GLASS
HONEYSETT

". . . And a worm, please."

Sempé

"The kiss of life?
To a goldfish?"

"Fascinating – I never realised Henry Moore had *a commercial period."*

"You ordered sole Picasso?"

"Apparently he used to work with dolphins."

"Can I see your licence?"

"They're rising well to that new ground-bait."

"If you want the rudiments of the upstream Grayling nymph, sir, it's a must."

"It was worth it! I got a half pounder."

"This is when decent tackle pays for itself."

"I don't recall a smile like that when you carried me over the threshold!"

"Not a nibble."

"They looked a lot bigger in the Morris Minor."

". . . And that's only the size of the fly."

*"Well, one way to tell the difference is that jetsam is usually **fresher** than flotsam."*

"It's Charlie – they sent him back."

NOEL FORD

"Oh, forget it – we'll have the steak!"

MAHOOD

"He's very good with children."

*"Guess what! We're now appearing in fish fingers –
anonymously, of course."*

Eric Burgin

Arnold WILES.

"Worse than sharks, Farrington –
wind-surfing soldier ants!"

"If it wasn't for these damn atomic submarines we could be using dynamite."

SAM'S FISHERIES
Eric Burgin

QUIET PETS LTD
Larry

"I don't know which irritates me more – pessimists or non-conformists."

"To be honest, I've seen better Marilyn Monroe look-alikes."

"That Pterophyllum Scalare's simply full of mischief."

"He's not still going on about the worm that got away?"

"He's survived a number of harpoon attacks."

"The Chairman is meticulous in checking the environment for possible pollution."

"Mind you, if it isn't a mirage we could be in big trouble."

"What bell? I didn't hear any bell."

ROCKET
thelwell.

"When did you last feed that goldfish?"

"It's not just the goldfish. He keeps puncturing the plastic."

"Your bath's ready, dear."

"I'm 59 and she's 64. You call that fresh?"

"Relax, blast you – relax!"

COOKSON

"Amazing – I never even knew there was a goldfish cemetery."

I'M GOING TO COUNT TO 10 AND I WANT EVERYONE TO TURN AROUND.
SCHWADRON

"A hundred and twenty-five quids worth of salmon tackle and he *takes them with a shillelagh."*

GRAHAM

"You spoil that goldfish, George!"

"He's the only trout I know who was tickled and lived to tell the tale."

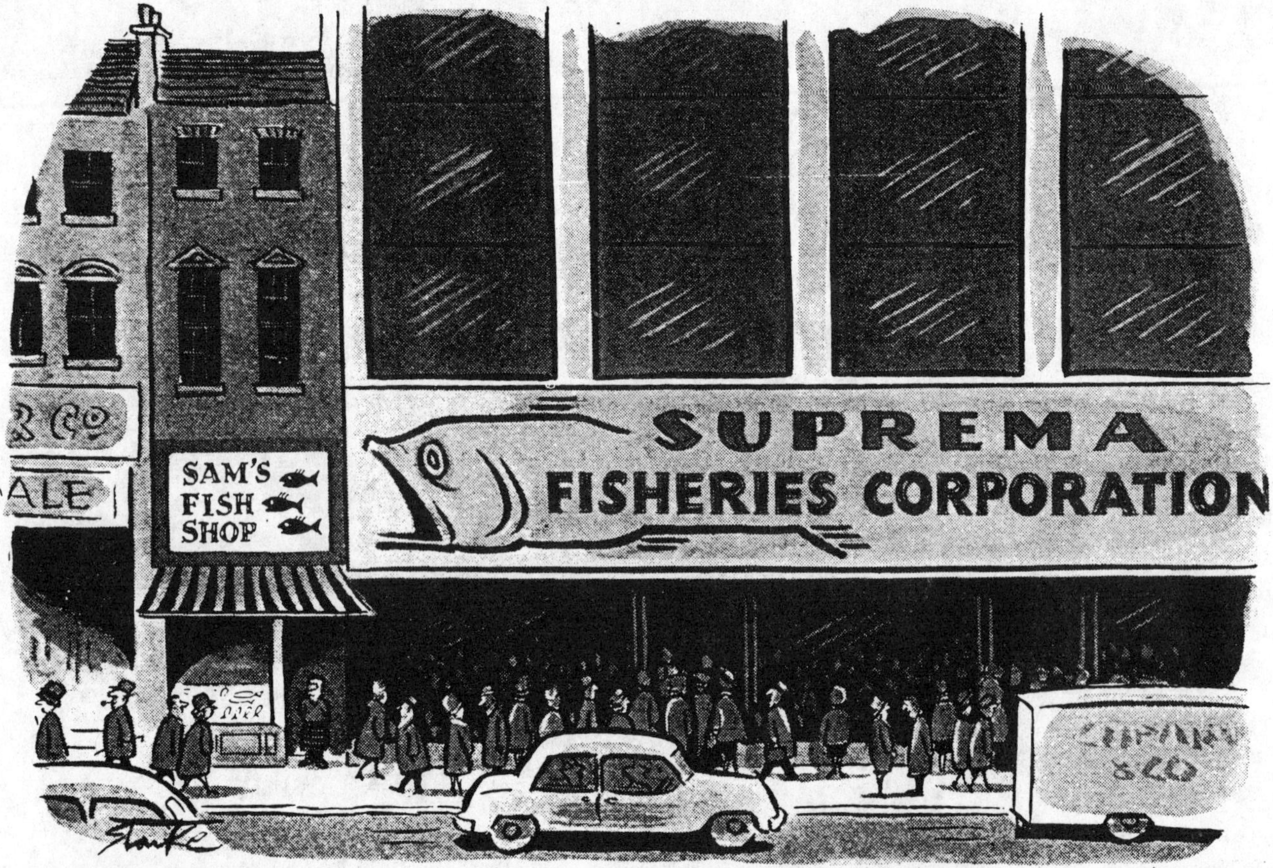
SAM'S
FISH
SHOP
SUPREMA
FISHERIES CORPORATION

"That's desperately uncool, you know. Sharks are totally last year's thing."

"He wasn't swimming anti-clockwise before we asked Mrs Candleberry to look after him."

"Here we go, Winston – excercise time."

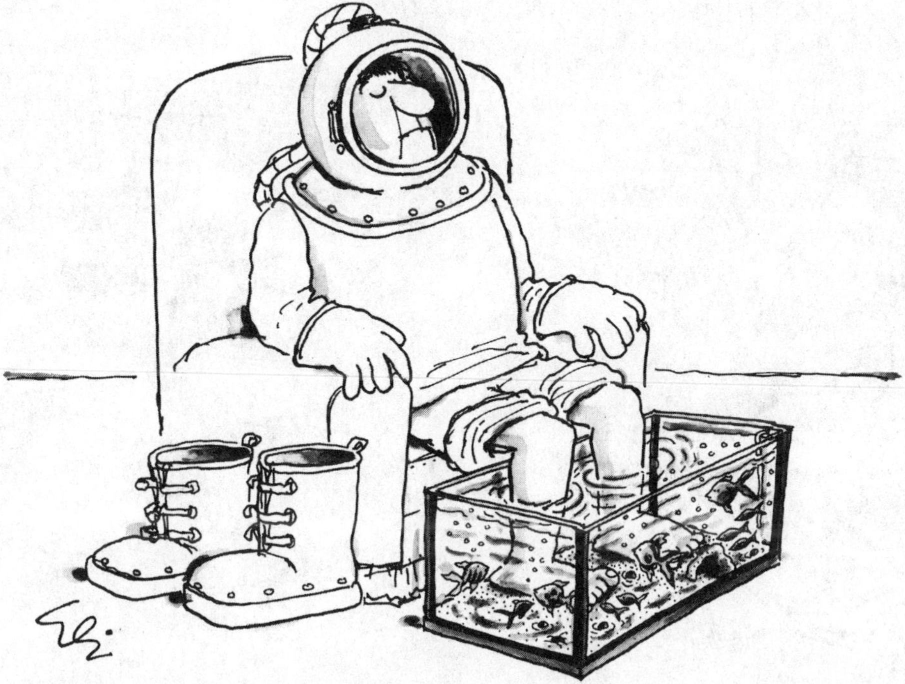

"Could you speed it up a little? The carp pond is almost fished out."

"Waiter, there's a fly in my soup."

"You have been granted a stay of execution until next month. Oysters don't come in till Setember."

"Two years tomorrow – and it's still a tadpole!"

"Motor racing been cancelled again?"

"Yes, I come here a lot – you'll find the trout all know me."

"Are you supposed to eat the boots?"

"I like to make a weekly call on…

…an unfortunate who lives on a pinch of food a day…

…who never leaves his tiny abode…

. . . and seldom sees a
cheerful face . . .

. . . so I give him a
weekly smile . . .

. . . and somehow it makes me
feel better."

HARGREAVES

"There won't be any peace now he's seen the ants' eggs."

"All right – I love you . . . I love you, I LOVE YOU! . . . O.K.?"

JOE'S FISH BAR
REGULARS ONLY
dredge

"These blasted students and their rag weeks!"

"It's that sort of thing that gets fishing a bad name."

"Perhaps he finds it easier to tread on them."

"... Target in Sector 3... speed 2 knots... angle of deflection 25°... who'd be a kingfisher?"

"What do you mean, you don't want it? With a little practice this could give you a lifetime's smoked salmon sandwiches."

"The mainland and step on it!"

thelwell

"Walkies!"

"So help me, Captain, it was a great white whale when I first saw it."

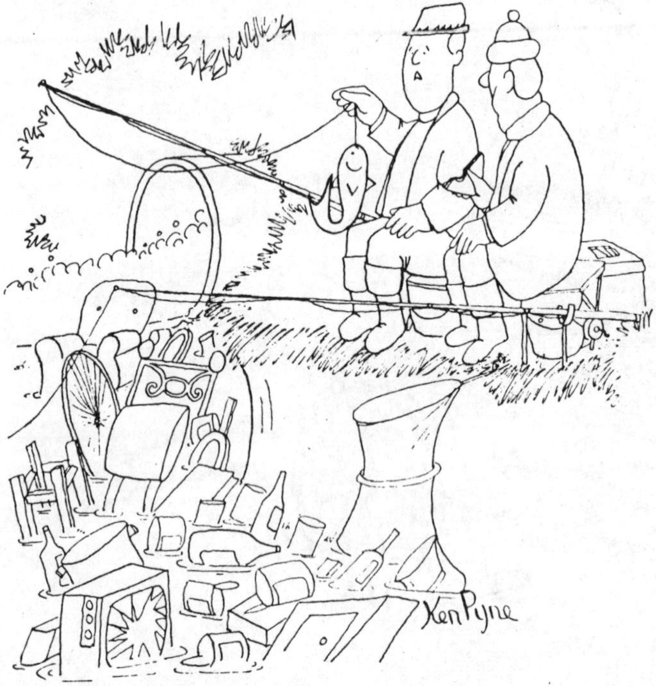

"You know something? I don't think I've got the heart to throw it back."

"Then when we got him home we couldn't face popping him into boiling water."

"Indeed I have suffered, sir – especially from fish poisoning."

"Mamma Mia! Is it Friday already?"

"Cap'n Ahab was always a damned unlucky fisherman!"

"Curiously restful, aren't they –
standing there with their mouths
shut like that."

"Just once more round the bowl, George – then we'll have to ask the lady to make up her mind."

"The ship's cat won't touch tinned meat."

JAWS
U CERT
CHILDRENS MATINEE VERSION

YES, I WANT TO BE
SAVED

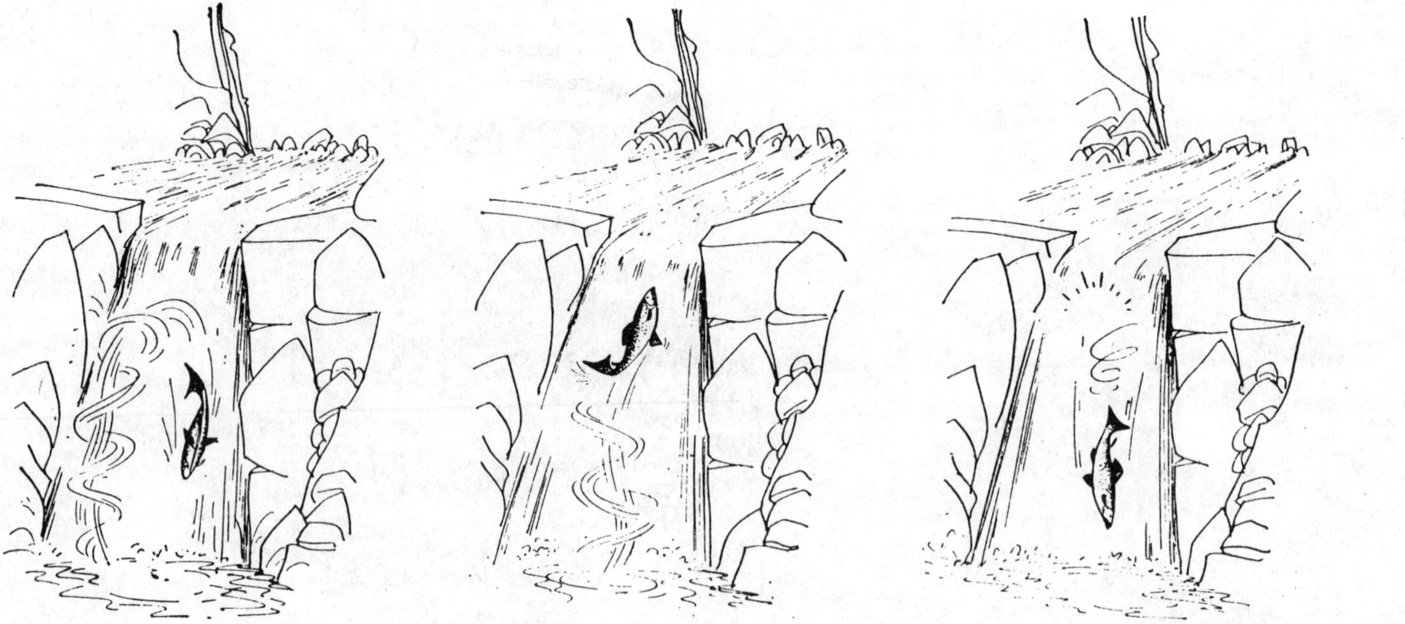

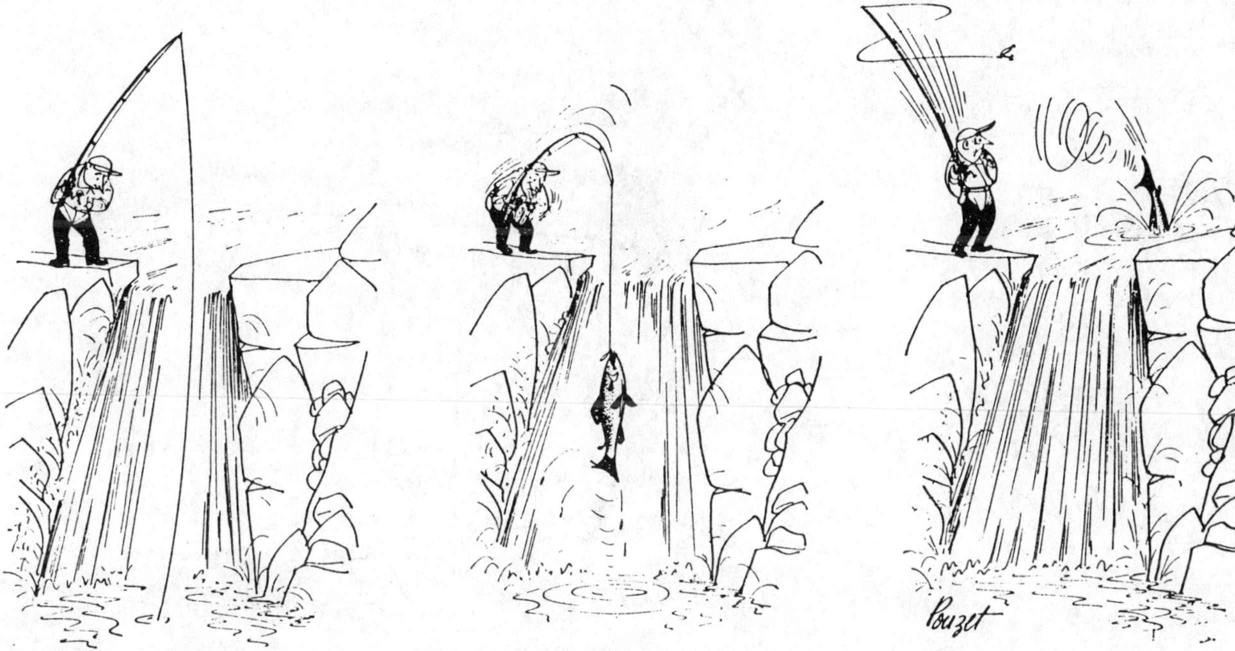
Pouzet

"They spend three years in the Atlantic and then run up the rivers to spawn."

"It's our only concession to the World Wildlife Fund."

"Remember now?"

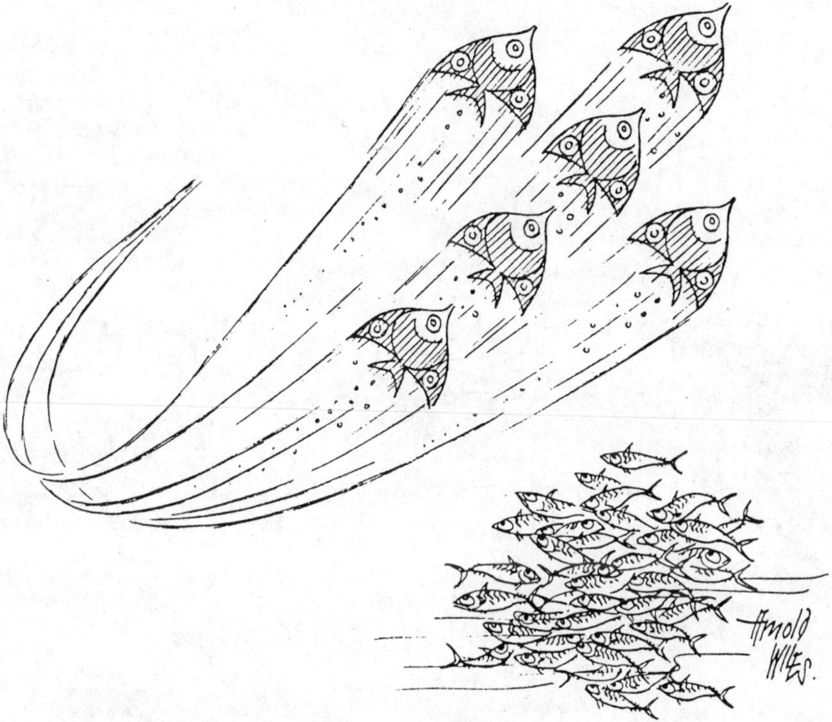
Arnold Wiles.

"I want something completely expressionless."

"It would have been enough to bless the fishing fleet."

"Oh no! – this time it's my turn to share it out!"

"No problem, kids. I am empowered to perform marriages at sea."

"Well, well! I'll serve an amusing little white wine!"

RIVER COTTAGE
SOLD
BY
BAGWORTH, COLBY
SMILLS & WINCH
A·E·BEARD

"Got the blighter!"

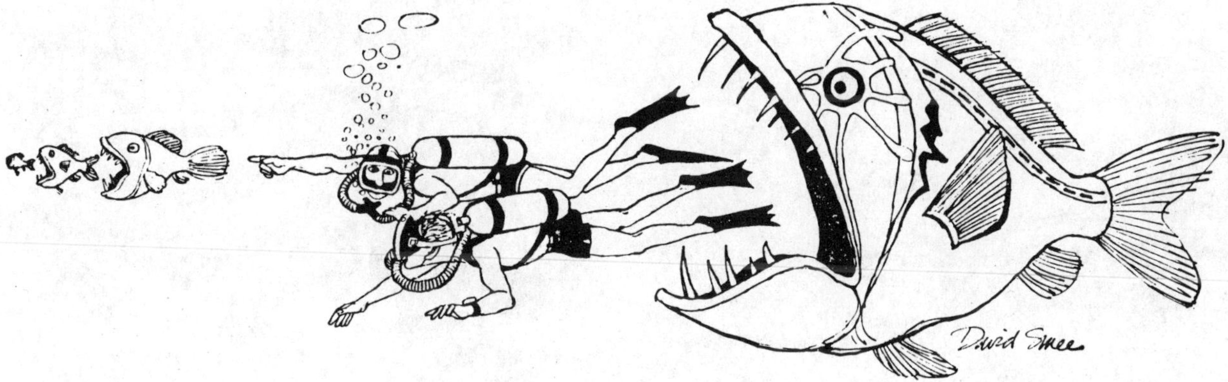

"Do you realise we are witnessing one of the eternal truths?"

"Madam, I suggest you turn away while my assistant removes the fish."

"Good luck, then – and here, you'll need this."

"*All they keep banging on about is* parental choice."

"Oh, no! Not the last of the goldfish!"

—Brookbank